To..

From..

D1389081

OTHER HELEN EXLEY GIFTBOOKS ON STRENGTH AND
COMFORT:

Thank You For Every Little Thing
Thoughts On Being Happy
Thoughts On Being At Peace
Wishing You Happiness
Words On Comfort
Words On Courage
Words On Hope
Words On Strength and Perseverance

Published simultaneously in 1999 by Exley Publications LLC in the
USA and Exley Publications Ltd in Great Britain.

12   11   10   9   8   7   6   5   4

Copyright © Helen Exley 1999
ISBN 1-86187-074-4

Edited and words selected by Helen Exley
Illustrated by Juliette Clarke
Printed and bound in Hungary

Exley Publications Ltd, 16 Chalk Hill, Watford, Herts WD1 4BN, UK.
Exley Publications LLC, 232 Madison Avenue, Suite 1206,
NY 10016, USA.

ACKNOWLEDGEMENTS: The publishers are grateful for permission to reproduce copyright
material. Whilst every reasonable effort has been made to trace copyright holders, the
publishers would be pleased to hear from any not here acknowledged. KAHLIL GIBRAN: From
The Prophet © 1923 Khalil Gibran, renewed 1951 by Administrators C.T.A. of Kahlil Gibran
Estate and Mary C. Gibran. ELIZABETH KÜBLER-ROSS: From Soul Gifts in Disguise reprinted
in Handbook for the Soul © 1995 by R. Carson and B. Shield published by Judy Piatkus Ltd.
and Little Brown & Company.

To someone special
IN TIMES
OF TROUBLE

Edited by Helen Exley
Illustrated by Juliette Clarke

I wish that I could ease your pain.

I hope these words will help to give

you courage and strength in the

difficult days ahead.

A HELEN EXLEY GIFTBOOK

EXLEY

NEW YORK • WATFORD, UK

Small sadnesses,
great tragedies,
link us all in love.

PAM BROWN, b.1928

...

YOU ARE NOT ALONE

Think of one thing. You are not alone. A million
million lives have known this pain – and found at
last a way to new tranquillity.

PAM BROWN, b.1928

...

Nothing happens to any man that he is not formed
by nature to bear.

MARCUS AURELIUS (121-180)

...

The bad news is: ours is an arduous, long and sometimes tedious journey through Cesspool Cosmos. And observe, it is a walk, not a sprint. The good news is: we are not alone on this demanding pilgrimage, which means that some folks we are traveling with make awfully good models to follow. So, follow them!

CHARLES R. SWINDOLL, FROM "LAUGH AGAIN"

. . .

Sorrow is the only one of the lower notes in the oratorio of our blessedness.

A. J. GORDON

. . .

Does the road wind up-hill all the way?
Yes, to the very end.
Will the day's journey take the whole day long?
From morn to night, my friend.

CHRISTINA ROSSETTI (1830-1894)

. . .

LESSONS IN LIFE

It is only when we have descended to the depths of

sorrow that we can understand the complexity of

being human,

feel for all other suffering living creatures,

honour courage –

and give understanding, kindness, and

companionship to those who need it.

PAM BROWN, b.1928

...

A man who suffers much, knows much; every day

brings him new wisdom.

EWE

...

Many of my AIDS patients discovered that the last year of their lives was by far their best. Many have said they wouldn't have traded the rich quality of that last year of life for a healthier body. Sadly, it is only when tragedy strikes that most of us begin attending to the deeper aspects of life.

ELIZABETH KÜBLER-ROSS, FROM "SOUL GIFTS IN DISGUISE"

...

Where there is sorrow, where there is pain, where there is fear – there loving kindness grows and flowers.

PAM BROWN, b.1928

...

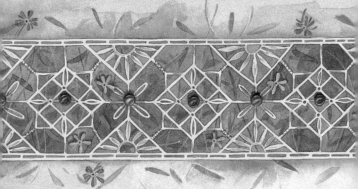

A MEDITATION

Deep in the soul, below pain, below all the
distraction of life, is a silence vast and grand – an
infinite ocean of calm, which nothing can disturb.
Nature's own exceeding peace, which "passes
understanding".

C.M.C. QUOTED BY R.M. BUCKE

...

Do not weep; do not wax indignant.
Understand.

BARUCH SPINOZA

...

Go with the pain, let it take you....
Open your palms and your body to the pain.
It comes in waves like a tide, and you must be
open as a vessel lying on the beach, letting
it fill you up and then, retreating, leaving
you empty and clear....
With a deep breath –
it has to be as deep as the pain – one reaches a kind
of inner freedom from pain, as though the pain
were not yours but your body's.

ANNE MORROW LINDBERGH, b.1906

...

THE SMALL JOYS

When the world seems huge and dark and
meaningless, focus on little things – sunlight
through leaves, a cat sprawled across your knees,
the taste of an apple, a dew bright spider's web.
Time for great wonders later
– now is the time for gentle comforts,
for friendly and familiar things.

PAM BROWN, b.1928

...

I think these difficult times have helped me to understand better than before how infinitely rich and beautiful life is in every way and that so many things that one goes around worrying about are of no importance whatsoever.

ISAK DINESEN (1885-1962)

...

Your success and happiness lie in you. External conditions are the accidents of life. The great enduring realities are love and service.
Joy is the holy fire that keeps our purpose warm and our intelligence aglow. Resolve to keep happy, and your joy and you shall form an invincible host against difficulty.

HELEN KELLER (1880-1968)

...

Birds sing after a storm; why shouldn't people feel as free to delight in whatever remains to them?

ROSE KENNEDY

...

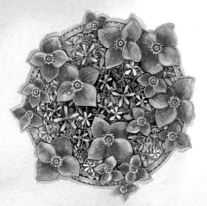

SUFFERING GROWS US

Out of every crisis comes the chance to be reborn,
to reconceive ourselves as individuals, to choose the
kind of change that will help us to grow and to
fulfil ourselves more completely.

NENA O'NEILL

. . .

In the depth of winter, I finally learned that within
me there lay an invincible summer.

ALBERT CAMUS (1913-1960)

. . .

It is only when one has been ill and has recovered that one can properly savour the glory of walking, breathing evenly, sleeping soundly, seeing clearly, waking to a new day.

PAM BROWN, b.1928

...

... we may measure our road to wisdom by the sorrows we have undergone.

BULWER

...

Once you have been confronted with a life-and-death situation, trivia no longer matters. Your perspective grows and you live at a deeper level.

MARGARETTA "HAPPY" ROCKEFELLER

...

Out of suffering have emerged the strongest souls, the most massive characters are seamed with scars....

E.H. CHAPIN

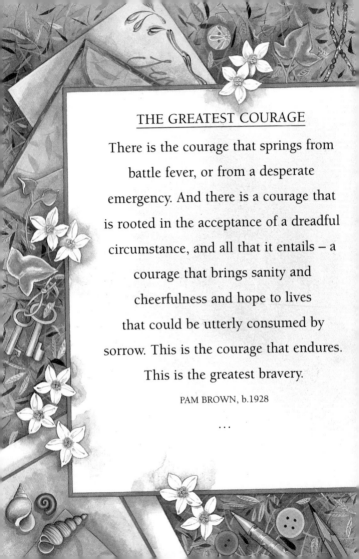

THE GREATEST COURAGE

There is the courage that springs from
battle fever, or from a desperate
emergency. And there is a courage that
is rooted in the acceptance of a dreadful
circumstance, and all that it entails – a
courage that brings sanity and
cheerfulness and hope to lives
that could be utterly consumed by
sorrow. This is the courage that endures.
This is the greatest bravery.

PAM BROWN, b.1928

…

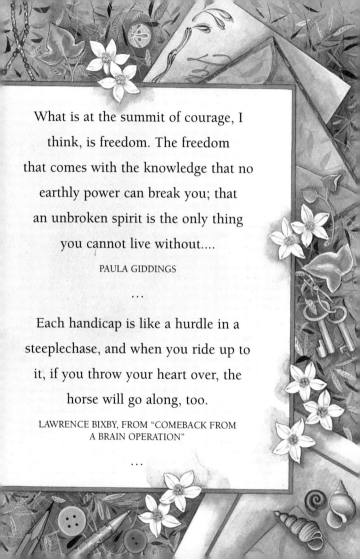

What is at the summit of courage, I
think, is freedom. The freedom
that comes with the knowledge that no
earthly power can break you; that
an unbroken spirit is the only thing
you cannot live without....

PAULA GIDDINGS

...

Each handicap is like a hurdle in a
steeplechase, and when you ride up to
it, if you throw your heart over, the
horse will go along, too.

LAWRENCE BIXBY, FROM "COMEBACK FROM
A BRAIN OPERATION"

...

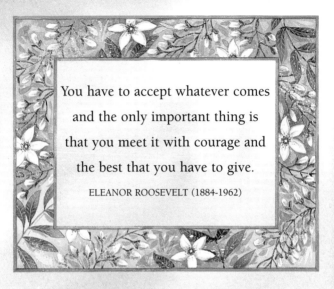

You have to accept whatever comes
and the only important thing is
that you meet it with courage and
the best that you have to give.

ELEANOR ROOSEVELT (1884-1962)

COURAGE THROUGH THE PAIN

Courage takes many forms. There is physical
courage, there is moral courage. Then there is a still
higher type of courage – the courage to brave pain,
to live with it, to never let others know of it and to
still find joy in life; to wake up in the morning with
an enthusiasm for the day ahead.

HOWARD COSELL, FROM "LIKE IT IS"

...

One of the best safeguards of our hopes is to be able
to mark off the areas of hopelessness and to
acknowledge them,
to face them directly, not with despair but with the
creative intent of keeping them from polluting all
the areas of possibility.

WILLIAM F. LYNCH

...

The only courage that matters is the kind that gets
you from one moment to the next.

MIGNON MCLAUGHLIN

...

You shall be free indeed when your days are
not without a care nor your nights without
a want and a grief.
But rather when these things girdle your life and yet
you rise above them naked and unbound.

KAHLIL GIBRAN (1883-1931)

...

IN DEEPEST TROUBLE

If the future seems overwhelming, remember that it
comes one moment at a time.

BETH MENDE CONNY

...

The best way out is always through.

ROBERT FROST (1874-1963)

...

Even as the stone of the fruit must break, that its
heart may stand in the sun, so must you know pain.

KAHLIL GIBRAN (1883-1931)

...

When the worst things happen I will remember that
I can and will handle them. I have been astounded
by the great strength in myself and in the suffering
people I've known.
I see now that there is unfathomable strength and
future joy for me, whatever awful problems come to
me. And, yes, that the same strength is yours too.

HELEN EXLEY

…

The solution is with you. It is as clear and bright as
a flame – but hidden from you by the swirling dark
of misery. Remember all the sweetness that has been
given you – and that still waits beyond the tumult.
It will take all your courage to withstand the
onslaught of despair.
But hold to quietness and hope.
Look to the centre of your being, the place of peace.

PAM BROWN, b.1928

HOPE

If it were not for hopes,

the heart would break.

THOMAS FULLER (1608-1661),
FROM "DRYAD SONG"

...

Become a possibilitarian. No matter

how dark things seem to be

or actually are, raise your sights and

see the possibilities – always see

them, for they're always there.

NORMAN VINCENT PEALE

...

Turn your face to the sun and

the shadows fall behind you.

MAORI PROVERB

...

It has never been, and never will be easy work! But the road that is built in hope is more pleasant to the traveler than the road built in despair, even though they both lead to the same destination.

MARION ZIMMER BRADLEY

...

The earth is empty.
The trees, once thick with blossom
stand dead against a bitter sky.
The streams are frozen.
But see – along the branches new buds appear
and greenness pushes through the ground
unnoticed.
Spring may be slow – but will at last return.

PAM BROWN, b.1928

...

It's better to light a candle than to
curse the darkness.

ELEANOR ROOSEVELT (1884-1962)

A GROWING STRENGTH

Know how sublime a thing is to suffer

and be strong.

HENRY WADSWORTH LONGFELLOW (1807-1882)

...

Although the world is full of suffering, it is also full

of the overcoming of it.

HELEN KELLER (1880-1968)

...

To endure is greater than to dare; to tire out

hostile fortune; to be daunted by no difficulty;

to keep heart when all have lost it – who can say

this is not greatness?

WILLIAM MAKEPEACE THACKERAY (1811-1863)

If I were asked to give what I consider the single most useful bit of advice for all humanity, it would be this: Expect trouble as an inevitable part of life, and when it comes, hold your head high, look it squarely in the eye and say, "I will be bigger than you. You cannot defeat me." ... Maintaining self-respect in the face of a devastating experience is of prime importance.

ANN LANDERS

...

Strengthen me by sympathizing with my strength, not my weakness.

A. BRONSON ALCOTT

...

THIS TOO WILL PASS

All shall be well, and all shall be well, and all
manner of thing shall be well.

JULIAN OF NORWICH

...

Weeping may endure for a night, but the morning
brings a shout of joy.

PSALMS 30.5

...

The shock of failure, of disappointments, of betrayal, hits like a physical blow. Breathless and blinded, you lose all contact with the life you lived till now – the ordinary life that seemed untouchable.

Hold fast. However impossible it seems that happiness and certainty will return – they will, they will. A thousand voices tell you so – speaking from hard experience.

PAM BROWN, b.1928

...

"This too will pass...." I was taught these words by my grandmother as a phrase that is to be used at all times in your life. When things are spectacularly dreadful; when things are absolutely appalling; when everything is superb and wonderful and marvellous and happy – say these four words to yourself. They will give you a sense of perspective....

CLAIRE RAYNER

...

HAPPINESS WILL ALWAYS BE WITH YOU

The world calls you back to life.

Listen.

The shrill of bird song.

A river breaking from the ice.

Rain after drought.

Sunshine after cloud.

PAM BROWN, b.1928

. . .

When one door closes another opens.

Expect that new door to reveal even greater

wonders and glories and surprises.

Feel yourself grow with every experience.

EILEEN CADDY

We must live through the dreary winter if we would value the spring. And the woods must be cold and silent before the robins sing. The flowers must be buried in darkness before they can bud and bloom. And the sweetest, warmest sunshine comes after the storm and gloom.

AUTHOR UNKNOWN

...

The pain passes, but the beauty remains.

PIERRE AUGUSTE RENOIR (1841-1919),
ON WHY HE STILL PAINTED DESPITE PAINFUL ARTHRITIS

...

Walk on a rainbow trail;

walk on a trail of song,

and all about you will be beauty.

There is a way out of every dark mist,

over a rainbow trail.

NAVAJO SONG

...